For Better
For Worse

by David Edgecombe

ISBN: 978-0-9908659-9-5

Library of Congress Control Number: 2015933864

Text copyright © 1973 David Edgecombe

Published by CaribbeanReads Publishing,

Basseterre, St. Kitts.

All rights reserved.

Printed in the USA

For Nicie, Eudora, and Dahlia

Table of Contents

Preface i

Productions xx

Cast xx

Characters xxi

Setting xxii

Act I 1

Act II 64

Preface

Setting the Stage

"In my next life," I told a friend on the phone, I'm going to choose another passion."

She asked, "How come?"

"August 2013 marked the 40th anniversary of my first play, *For Better For Worse*," I said, "And if you total all the money I made from playmaking over the years, you couldn't get $10,000." She laughed and laughed and laughed. And I'm sure if she thinks of it now she will throw back her head and laugh again. She was a trained accountant but had switched to become a building contractor. It paid better. For her, my story couldn't add up.

A year later at the Nature Island Literary Festival and Book Fair in Dominica, I relayed this anecdote to my old friend, Dorbrene 'Fatz' O'Marde, who was also staging a play at the festival.

He said, "Well boy, that's $10,000 more than me." We had a good laugh, unmarred by bitterness. I think.

Friends have asked, "Why do it?" in a tone that says, 'you must be crazy or stupid, maybe both.' I understand the sentiment but never take issue with it because there's no good answer. Except, perhaps, to say along the way good things do happen.

For instance, CaribbeanReads, a new publishing company offered in the summer of 2013 to edit and publish all of my plays. The company is headed by Carol Ottley-Mitchell, herself an author of children's and young adult's books. I grabbed the offer especially after it was agreed I would write a preface to each play discussing the circumstances under which it had been written and staged. It would amount to a personal odyssey that should provide some insight into Caribbean Theatre from the late 1900s to the early 21st Century. In an area of the world where scant attention is paid to recording such histories there's bound to be value here. Let's do it.

Early Days

By fifteen I felt I knew more about drama production than anyone at the Montserrat Secondary School (MSS), if not the whole of Montserrat.

It wasn't all conceit. Since I was about eight I had been mimicking the smartmen, drunks, and petty scoundrels who enlivened the streets of Plymouth. My older sister Eudora put together a skit with me in it to entertain friends at home that somehow made it into a performance at MSS. Not long after, I began staging improvised skits with my schoolmates and soon graduated to writing my own.

More significantly, I had attended two drama workshops put on by the University of the West Indies to train youngsters from different islands in voice and diction, movement, acting, writing, stage management, set building, props, costumes, you name it. The workshops were organized around three or four plays that were staged at the end. We learned through doing.

The first I attended was in Dominica in 1965. I don't know if any of us participants understood we were continuing a legacy of theatre training that began in the early 1950s with the late Errol Hill, freshly returned from his theatre studies in London. He was employed by UWI and traveled through the English speaking Caribbean, often, I learned, with Noel Vaz, promoting and teaching drama as well as advocating for the writing of indigenous Caribbean plays. Eventually this groundbreaking work led to a significant collection of one act plays (the Red and White Series), medium length-plays (Yellow and White) and full-length plays (Blue and White) that served a fledging Caribbean theatre well. I believe for his pioneering work, Hill should be considered the father of Caribbean Theatre.

I didn't know that history when I attended that first workshop, but it didn't matter. It was enough to be in the gathering with others who were as anxious as I to learn about theatre. I didn't know either that the program had changed drastically. Instead of Hill, Noel Vaz, or both travelling to different islands, Noel Vaz and Dennis Scott of Jamaica, and Daphne Hackett of Barbados organized workshops on one island and brought students in from other islands.

One huge advantage of this new model was that it helped forge a network of Caribbean theatre people. It was at my first of these that I met Alwin Bully and we have been friends and in regular contact since. To my best knowledge, we are the only two attendees still active in theatre today.

Brian Meade, a lifelong friend who recently headed the Dominica Broadcasting Services (DBS), was the only other person from Montserrat who attended. Soon after we returned, we started the Montserrat Secondary School Dramatic Society (MSSDS) with him as president and me as stage manager.

The second UWI Theatre workshop was in Antigua in 1968, at which time I was president of the

MSSDS. We brought a play to that workshop, *The Goose and The Gander*, I believe, by Wilfred Redhead of Grenada. It was from the Red & White series published by the Extra Mural Department of UWI that had resulted from Errol Hill's efforts to promote the writing of Caribbean plays.

I don't remember many details about the workshop, except that it taught me one of the most valuable lessons I learned about theatre. I've recounted the experience before in this way:

Minutes before we were to perform at the University Centre in Antigua, there was an electricity blackout. A tall elegant woman whose name I don't remember said, "Get the actors ready, you're going on."

I said, "Without lights?"

She said, "Just get yourselves ready."

I was adamant. "We're not going on without lights."

"And what should we say to the hundreds of people sitting out there in the audience?"

There was indeed a large audience in the open-air auditorium with only the light of the moon to see by. I shrugged.

"Listen young man," she said, "The one immutable law of theatre is, the show must go on. We will use flambeaux, or searchlights or catch fire flies in a bottle, if we have to, but the show must go on."

And so it did, with the stage lit by flambeaux. Shortly before the play ended the electric lights came back on and ruined the warm, cozy embrace we were in with the audience. This lesson has served me well.

***

The last and grandest of these early workshops was in Jamaica in 1970. It brought together dramatists and dancers and singers from the region at the Creative Arts Centre, UWI, Mona. There were two other attendees from Montserrat: Edith Bellot Allen, a wonderful singer and the faculty member in charge of the MSS's Glee Club, who was with the choral segment, and Willie 'Kinnie' O'Garro, who I believe attended the dance segment and whose contribution to the performing arts in Montserrat is beyond measure. He had been in Jamaica for some months training in dance and drumming.

Members of all three disciplines did calisthenics together each morning, had all our meals together, and spent the rest of the time working in our own disciplines.

The campus was abuzz with creative energy. Everywhere somebody was painting or drawing or playing music. It was what we called in those days a nice vibe. It was what made the workshop special.

One of the highlights was a session with the great Louise Bennett. I recall being mesmerized by her, her smile and her laughter. I was amazed at how relaxed she was—though bursting with energy, how in control of herself and space and ultimately of us, and how easy and delightful she made performing seem.

Rex Nettleford sightings were regularly reported. And the women were always trying to out-lament each other about how handsome he was. I remember seeing him, but don't remember hearing him speak (which now seems unusual) and we knew of course he was the founding leader and chief choreographer of the National Dance Theatre Company (NDTC).

We learned he was a champion for the arts and working people of Jamaica and the Caribbean.

Many years later, Dennis Scott, the first head of the Jamaica School of Drama who moved to Yale School of Drama to teach directing, told me a Nettleford story. He said Rex once went to a meeting with some big name American artists and officials who at the end of the meeting rode away in limos or fancy cars while Nettleford left on foot. I asked what that meant and Dennis, as he was inclined to do, stared into space and said nothing more. I could only guess at his meaning, perhaps that it was ironic Nettleford with his superior intellect and talent was the one who had to walk, or that Nettleford's artistic and intellectual measure could never be taken by material trappings or that the world's reward system is skewered. Who knows?

One night, workshop attendees went to a performance of Samuel Becket's *Waiting For Godot*. Vladimir was played by Lloyd Record, a Jamaican who had studied acting in London and Estragon by Tom Cross, an Englishman teaching at UWI who would remain active in Caribbean theatre for many years. Just before it got started two Rastafarians came into the theatre and sat in the front row.

It was my first time seeing Theatre of the Absurd. The show was captivating, but in class the next morning the presence of the Rastas dominated our discussions. The diffusion of Rastafarian philosophy and lifestyles to the rest of the Caribbean and the world had not yet taken place. Rastas were seen as a strange sect, maybe hostile, and definitely at the fringe of Jamaican society. In six years, after the release of

The Harder They Come in 1972 and the return of hundreds of students from Jamaica to the Eastern Caribbean with dreadlocks, reggae music, and the
sacramental, and not so sacramental, smoking of the
"weed of wisdom", "Rasta" would become the Caribbean's most powerful artistic, cultural, philosophical,
and religious force of the latter part of the 20th Century.

Did the presence of the two Rastafarians at the
play signal to us at the workshop there was a movement churning in Jamaica, saying things about culture
and identity and Africa than our universities could
never say, and that would have far greater resonance
throughout the region than any absurdist play?

At that workshop I was cast in *The Rape of Fair
Helen* by Stanley French of St. Lucia who was working
in Jamaica as an engineer. The play was directed by
Dennis Scott, from whom I learned much just by
observing him work. He was highly organized, always
prepared, focused, and he loved to experiment. For
instance, he had three women play the role of Helen,
all on stage at the same time, each responding differ-
ently at any given moment. The idea, I think, was to
show we're all made up of different personalities that
vie for dominance in the decision making process. I
don't know how effective that device was, as I was
acting in the play and couldn't assess it well, but I
never saw it used again.

Dennis was sometimes brutal. He pushed one of
the Helens, a young Jamaica teacher, at rehearsal one
night until she collapsed in uncontrollable tears. She
told me after she hated him, felt belittled and didn't
know if she could continue. But she did, all the way

through to the performance. I often wonder what became of her.

Stanley French was a regular visitor at rehearsals but always stayed in the background. He and Dennis seemed to have a healthy respect for each other. I didn't interact with him then, but would come to know him well in the years ahead. He was what the Caribbean calls high-strung, but he had an infectious laugh and a good sense of humor. I made time to see him whenever I visited St. Lucia. On one such occasion he was in the process of editing and publishing all of his writings. He told me then, the world mistakenly has it that Derek (Walcott) is St. Lucia's playwright, but it will come to see Derek is St. Lucia's poet and Stanley French her playwright. We mourned his passing on November 10, 2010.

The Montserrat Theatre Group

Shortly after I returned from Jamaica, the Montserrat Theatre Group (MTG) was formed. It was the first adult group dedicated exclusively to putting on plays, no doubt because it was held, if not written, that smart adults should not over-indulge in trite activities such as "playing". I had finished high school and was working as an announcer at Radio Montserrat but couldn't see myself giving up theatre.

One of the first plays MTG staged was the world premiere of *Pushing Up You Hand, Pushing Up You Hand and Bowling a Straight Ball*, or *Dropping Out is Violence*, by A. E. Markham, who was called Archie by all. He left Montserrat with his family as a boy to live in England. He returned for a visit in 1970 by way of Guyana, Trinidad, and St. Vincent in an effort no doubt to experience more of the Caribbean. In Guyana he worked for weeks as a laborer helping to build the Demarara Highway. In Trinidad he did a stint with the Trinidad Theatre Workshop founded by Derek Walcott, and in St. Vincent he directed one of his plays, an experience that must have been memorable for him. He told me, "The actresses arrived for the performance dressed in their Sunday best. When I asked them to change into their costumes they said, 'You must be mad if you think we're going on stage in those rags'."

One night Noel Vaz showed up at a rehearsal of *Pushing Up You Hand* and in the middle of it cried out, "Archie, Archie, you're making it sound as if all there is in life is sex and money."

Archie, deadpan, said, "And it isn't?"

"Of course not! Look at Franklin Roosevelt. In spite of all his money he spent most of his life in a wheelchair."

"If he didn't have money he would have been dead."

Vaz threw his hands in the air and walked away. Archie went on with the rehearsal as if nothing had happened.

Pushing Up You Hand... was an absurdist play. Those of us who acted in it, confessed we didn't understand what it was about, but the audience loved it and it was a huge success. We were invited to bring the play to Antigua, but one of the actresses became a born-again Christian and withdrew from the play. I tried my damnedest to get her to change her mind, but she wouldn't budge. All of us in the play were disappointed. Archie remained dispassionate.

***

My mother was the greatest storyteller I know. She didn't think of herself as that, and if anyone should have asked her to tell a story in public she most certainly would have declined. But regularly after super and especially after the big Sunday meal she regaled us with stories. Seemingly without pre-planning she would transform into the characters she was talking about—whether it was Moses confronting the Red Sea, or our deceased father denouncing the notion of a jumbie-name, or our dog Laddie showering her with love—imbuing her stories with life.

Such was the tapestry in which I became an adult. Theatre was alive at my home, on the streets of Plymouth, and everywhere else. I got to travel and meet other students and actors, directors, artists and writers. Some were exceptional craftsmen. Instructors at the workshops seemed to want to forge a pan-Caribbean theatre. That idea never left me.

Those workshops and other theatre experiences gave me grounding. So I left for college confident I knew my way around theatre and all I didn't know, I could learn. Theatre was my turf. Creativity was my rod and staff.

College Years

I arrived in Canada in August 1971 on a Canadian International Development Aid (CIDA) scholarship to study Radio and Television Arts. I attended Lethbridge Community College, in Lethbridge Alberta for the first year and Niagra Colledge in Weland Ontario for the second.

That year in Lethbridge was one of my most enjoyable years in Canada and the year in which I was the most Canadian. It was also my first time being alone, and I had to come to grips with aloneness. Not loneliness, aloneness. This became most acute when I took a bus ride to Montreal to spend the Christmas of 1971 with old friends from Montserrat. The journey lasted almost three days and had a seminal effect on me.

After I had read till my eyes were blurry, then looked out the bus window for hours at nothing but fields of snow, I had no place else to look but inward. Aloneness allows you to do that without distraction and I connected with a 'me' I had some inkling of, but barely knew. I questioned my life, my past actions, motives, and existence. I looked at the people I grew up with, seeing even their warts without flinching. I had an early notion the real world was vastly different than what we learned in Church and school and that most times things were not what they appeared to be. I peered into this and recognized we were conditioned to question nothing when in fact we should be questioning everything; that gross intolerance frequently masqueraded as conventional wisdom; that conventional wisdom was often the chief inhibitor of knowledge; that ugly sentiment and prejudice and pettiness and superstition were stunting us. These were seditious thoughts in my neighborhood that right-minded people knew not to entertain. Well, on that bus ride, trapped in my aloneness, I entertained them. I threw the doors open wide and welcomed them in. Those doors never closed again.

I got onto that bus in Lethbridge and got off in Montreal a different person

***

1972 brought word of the first Caribbean Festival of the Creative Arts (CARIFESTA) to be held in Guyana from August 25 to September 15. More than 30 Caribbean and Latin American countries were to be represented by over 1000 creative artists presenting music, dance, drama, folk art, painting, sculpture, photography and literature. There was to be drama of every kind from musical productions to comedy, drama, fantasy, ritual, history, folk plays and legends.

CARIFESTA came and went and was reportedly a huge success. Montserrat performed Big Business, a play by Vincent Browne, who was principal of the Montserrat Secondary School for my first two years there. He had written over 15 one act plays for the Montserrat Defense Force. Dominica performed *Speak Brother Speak* by Daniel Cauderion, a playwright I had not heard about, directed by my old friend Alwin Bully. Antigua presented *Prince Klaus* by Oliver Flax, another playwright I didn't know. The bus was leaving and I was not on board. What was I doing in Canada? I had not yet written a single line of a play. I didn't even have an idea for a play.

There was good reason for this. I had made a conscious decision four years earlier never to write another play.

The first play I actually wrote, as opposed to slapped together in rehearsal, was a farce called *The Fool and the Ass*. I stole the idea from a skit with the same title, performed by a visiting Antigua Police Company. Mine was an attempt to maul a Corporal Charles who denied me a driver's learning permit at thirteen, loudly assuring me he would cut my ass and send me home for Miss Belle (my mother) to finish the job if I wasn't out of his face and the police station in 10 seconds. It turned out to be a hit at my high school. More significantly, it got me a 'commission' to write a play about a failed slave rebellion in Montserrat on St. Patrick's Day, 1768.

Two of our leading scholars, Howard Fergus and George Irish, unearthed this story while doing research in England. They gave it to me in a brief paragraph and asked if I could write a play about it. Grenada, then headed by Sir Eric Gairy, had invited the other Caribbean islands to a grand cultural exposition and they wanted to present the play as part of Montserrat's contribution.

Nobody liked the first version, so I wrote a second version that everybody liked but I didn't like too much. The play was never staged. For any number of reasons, Montserrat carried a contingent of only five to Grenada in which I was included as my reward for writing the play.

The fact that the play was not performed did not bother me. The real issue was that the process of writing it was so painful it caused me to swear off of playwriting.

Some 25 years later, a copy of the script turned up at a book fair in Montserrat. By then, I had no copy of the play. Neither did my mother or any of my three sisters. Neither did my school or any of my teachers. The copy was loaned to the fair by Hans and Edith Herman, a couple from America who were said to have survived Auschwitz and ran a bookshop in Plymouth that I frequented when I was a boy.

My cousin Yvonne Weeks, now a lecturer at the University of the West Indies, sent me a copy soon after she directed the first ever performance of it, which I hope will be the only one. I read about half a page and couldn't continue—it was so horrible.

The poet Edward 'Kamau' Brathwaite told me years later at CARIFSTA in St. Kitts he knew exactly what the problem had been because he had confronted it himself.

"I knew, or could imagine," he told me, "What the slaves' work day was like, whether in the field, the boiler room, or the great house. But at the end of the day when he got to his hut, I had no idea what happened there. Until I took the trouble to find out, I couldn't write authentically about slave, or plantation, life."

Kamau was right, but I didn't have the benefit of his insight when I was writing the play. So I struggled through a painful journey that seemed like writing with one drop of blood at a time and I didn't want to go back there.

Because of this experience, I had taken myself out of the playwriting pool and now that I wanted back in, I had no idea what to write.

Then one winter morning around two, I awoke with an idea. I reflected on the characters, situations they were in and after time a storyline emerged. I pulled out my old Olivetti portable typewriter and started pounding away. The writing process was not much easier than before, but guided by instinct I pushed on until I finished the first scene. I asked my roommate, Tom Pagonius, a Canadian of Greek descent, for his feedback on this first scene.

When he handed the script back to me he said, "This is all words, you have no action."

"What you mean?" I asked.

"You should scrap all of it and start over."

I didn't touch the script again for weeks. When it eventually drew me back in, I proceeded with great caution. That casual assessment had shaken me almost to the point of numbness. I decided never to show the script to another person till it was done. Since then, I've never shown any part of an unfinished first draft to anyone.

I also decided that when the script was finished I would try to get it staged in Montserrat, certain if the audience there was going to throw anything it would be rotten tomatoes rather than stones. I was more comfortable with that but remained nervous and uncertain of the play all the way to opening night.

The Home Ground

Montserrat scheduled its first Alliougana Arts Festival for August 1973. It was to be a cultural exhibition of song, dance, drama, literature, folk creations, arts, and crafts. This was the brainchild of Dr. George Irish, who in 1970 returned from the Department of Spanish, UWI Jamaica, to head the UWI Extra Mural Centre. What he accomplished in three years was nothing short of a cultural and academic revolution. He encouraged those in Montserrat who had gone to secondary school but had not matriculated to finish up at the Centre so they could go on to university. Many who were languishing in close to dead end, low-paying jobs took up the challenge, completed university and established new, much better paying careers. He encouraged all the good singers, many of whom had turned into couch potatoes, to join Emerald Community Singers, a new choral group he founded.

He supported and encouraged the Montserrat Theatre Group. He arranged for Willie 'Kinnie' O'Garro, a great dancer and drummer to teach drumming and dancing at the University Centre. With the help of Howard Fergus and Edith Bellot Allen and others, great things were made to happen.

George also founded, with Jeddy Fenton (a writer), the Montserrat Allied Workers Union (MAWU), and was working with Vereen Thomas (who later became a playwright) to make into a strong organization for workers. That coupled with his cultural revolution would get Dr. Irish chased into exile by then Chief Minister P. Austin Bramble and his younger brother Howell.

All of this must have been brewing when I returned to Montserrat for the first Alliougana Arts Festival in the summer of 1973 but I didn't see it. I had no notion that before the end of the year a snap election would be called to "stop racism", George would be gone, and there would never be another Alliougana Arts Festival. What I saw was a Montserrat awakened and energized, as I had never seen it. I fed into that and focused on getting *For Better For Worse* staged.

We held the first reading and the general response was positive, with John Wilson, businessman, former cricketer and former actor, the notable exception. He objected to the 'bad words' in the play. What bad words? 'Damn' and 'shit?' 'Ass and self-righteous assholes?' We butted heads at length but I refused to change a word.

I didn't at this point have a title for the play because nothing I came up with seemed appropriate.

But the producers needed one for advertising and promotion so they kept pushing me.

Sonja Osborne, George's administrative assistant, said, "David, we're out of time, you have to come up with a title."

I said, "I've been trying for months with no success."

"Okay," she said, "What's the play about?"

I said it was about two young people who want to have a child out of wedlock, live together and raise the child together without getting married, but find themselves in a huge struggle with the girl's mom and the guy's dad who insist that cannot happen.

"Easy," she said. "Call it 'For Better For Worse.'"

I knew immediately there was no better title.

We began rehearsing with Edith Roach as Sandra; Dorothy Greenaway as Ann; Gus White as Derek; Leslie Kelsick as Andrew; Wilfred Francis as James; Glinis Hunter as Molly; John O'Garro as Joe and Edith Kirnon as Carol. Two weeks into our five-week schedule the same John Wilson who didn't like the 'bad words' called me to his office. He said I had offended him by putting a young lady who was under his guardianship in my filthy play and he was withdrawing her forthwith.

The actor being withdrawn was Edith Roach, beautiful and talented but still at high school. I tried to get Wilson to change his mind, pointing out that as someone who had himself been in theatre he must know how much his action would hurt the production. He said he didn't see how I could think he would give permission for this child he was responsible for to play a role in which she wanted to have a child out of wedlock and live with a man without being married to him. I told him it was a play for God's sake, a play! He told me I knew full well that Montserrat often branded people for life with the roles they played. She had to withdraw from the play and that was that.

I went searching for a replacement actor and found Jacqui Fredrick, equally beautiful and talented, but with little or no acting experience. We thought it best to have her play the less demanding role of Carol and move Edith Kirnon, who was playing Carol, into the lead role of Sandra. Rehearsals continued until one night with less than a week to go before opening, Wilfred Francis, the actor playing James Llewellyn Wellington, didn't show for rehearsal. We quickly learned he had been rushed to emergency for an appendectomy. The operation was successful and he was recuperating in hospital, out of danger. He was also out of the play and we were a few days away from opening, short of a lead actor.

I thought, surely the gods are punishing me, but above that thought, I could hear that elegant lady from Antigua screaming in my head, "The show must go on!"

Junior Lewis, one of my buddies, came to the rescue. We had gone through high school in the same form and had performed together many times. He immediately understood our predicament and accepted the challenge of saving the production. In two days he learned all the lines as we rehearsed flat out. Fortunately, the role of James may as well have been written for him.

We opened on schedule to a full, lively house. The actors were charged. They opened well and the scene in which James almost succeeds in seducing Ann was played to within perfection. Junior had to maneuver Dorothy across stage onto a chair that flattened out into a bed as they both faked innocence of what was happening. Brief as the scene was, it laid bare the hypocrisy the play is about. The audience got it like a whiplash and screamed with guilty delight. There was raucous applause at the end.

That opening night was victory. It was validation. It put to rest the doubts and misgivings I had harbored for months. It answered the all-important question: Can I really write a play? I've heard that people manage to experience delirious happiness only two or three times in their life. The premiere performance of *For Better For Worse* was one of mine.

David

22 February, 2015

NB

I must point out the following correction: In previous editions of *For Better For Worse*, Irene Bramble is credited with creating the role Ann Forgerty. Dorothy Greenaway was in fact the first person to play the role. I thank Edith Kirnon for pointing this out and Gus White for confirming it. And I apologize to Dorothy and Irene for my error. -de

Productions

For Better For Worse was first produced by the Montserrat Theatre Group as part of the Alliouagana Arts Festival, Montserrat, on July 18, 1973, at the University Center. It was directed by the author, and earned him the award for best director that year, with the following cast:

Cast in Order of Appearance

SANDRA FORGERTY	Edith Kirnon
ANN FORGERTY	Dorothy Greenaway
DEREK WELLINGTON	Gus White
ANDREW FORGERTY	Leslie Kelsick
JAMES WELLINGTON	Josephus Lewis
MOLLY	Glinnis Hunter
JOE	John O'Garro
CAROL	Jacqui Frederick

Characters

SANDRA FORGERTY	A young graduate teacher.
ANN FORGERIY	Sandra's mother; a house wife.
DEREK WELLINGTON	Sandra's boyfriend; a university student.
ANDREW FORGERTY	Sandra's father; a top level civil servant.
JAMES WELLINGTON	Derek's father; a Minister of Government.
MOLLY	James' maid.
JOE	A taxi driver.
CAROL	A school teacher.

Setting

The play is set on Montserrat in the early 1970's.

ACT ONE, SCENE ONE

The Forgerty's living room

The room is furnished somewhat better than the average middle income West Indian living room. Down left is an exit leading to the kitchen. Down right an exit leading to the bedrooms and up stage centre is the front door leading to the street. There is a centre table, a couch, and an easy chair with a side table close by. A radio must be part of the set. There could also be a TV, side-lights, and pictures making up the decor, but the stage should not be over-crowded.

ACT ONE, SCENE TWO

The Wellington's back veranda

A veranda table and two or three veranda chairs. Left, a big "sleeping chair." Upstage a table with a telephone on it. A door leads into the house. Another door leads directly to James' bedroom. Entering from the audience is entering from the back yard.

ACT TWO, SCENE ONE

The Forgerty's living room

For Better
For Worse

by David Edgecombe

ACT I

Scene 1

(When the lights come up the stage is empty. Sandra enters from bedroom [right] with a pile of exercise books. She walks over to the easy chair and places the books on the side table. Then she goes to the radio and switches it on. A "hot tune" is playing and she does a little dance as she goes back to the easy chair and sits. She starts marking books. In a little while, she puts down book and clutches her belly in pain. At this point Ann enters from kitchen)

ANN

I can't hear my ear in the place for all these benna songs, every minute.

(She switches the dial to a religious station)

There. Listen to something decent for a change.

(She looks at Sandra suspiciously)

You feeling bad again, Sandra?

SANDRA

(She tries to brighten-up)

Oh no, Mommy. I'm just concentrating on what I'm doing. I'm trying to finish marking these books before Derek comes over.

ANN

Well, don't let me keep you.

ANN (Continued)

(She goes back into the kitchen, pausing at door to look at Sandra)

(Sandra goes back to marking books. In a short while she puts down the book, switches off the radio and lies down on the couch)

ANN

(From off)

What you take it off for?

(She comes back in)

I want to listen.

(She sees to Sandra lying on the couch)

You feeling sick again Sandra?

SANDRA

I'm alright, Mommy. Don't worry your head.

ANN

How you mean you're alright? I didn't know you're a doctor.

SANDRA

I don't feel so good, but it's nothing to make a big fuss about.

ANN

(Coming over and examining her with hands)

Which part of you hurting?

SANDRA

(Pushing her off)

Just sit down and relax, Mommy. I tell you it's nothing.

ANN

I don't care what you say. If this goes on I'm calling Dr. O'Garro to look at you.

SANDRA

Oh Christ!

ANN

Something must be wrong with you. Last week you missed two days of school. Since when you ever missing two days of school in one week? You wouldn't eat a thing and you're so poory, it looks like you're withering away. I even had to ask them to pray for you at church.

SANDRA

(Getting up)

Look here, Mommy. See? I told you I'll be alright. There's nothing wrong with me. I've been working hard and I'm just a little run down. That's all.

ANN

All I'm saying is that the best thing to do...

SANDRA

Okay, Mommy I'll visit the doctor, I'll visit the doctor. Where's Daddy?

ANN

I couldn't tell you my child.

SANDRA

Isn't this his night for bridge?

ANN

Oh yes. He's probably out playing cards with Mr. Wellington. The Honorable James Llewellyn Wellington. I wonder if all these dreadful things people say about him could be true. You sure you feeling okay?

SANDRA

I'm fine, Mommy. What dreadful things?

ANN

The usual. How he's always interfering with his secretaries and things like that. And how he's going around now with some little girl half his age.

SANDRA

People always chatting about what's not their business. I'm sure nothing go like half the things they say.

ANN

Old people say you never see fire without smoke.

SANDRA

And if he even has a young girl, what's wrong with that? It might do him some good.

ANN

I don't believe it. I couldn't bring myself to believe such a thing about Mr. Wellington.

(Pause)

ANN (Continued)

You think anything could go so for true?

SANDRA

Why don't you ask him when you see him again?

ANN

I can't do that! But Mr. Wellington is too much of a fine, upstanding man to be involved in that kind of thing, anyhow. And a good politician too. Just this morning they said on the radio that he's going to Guyana tomorrow. Just look at that. Going abroad to represent his island again, and at a big time conference on Federation besides. What a man. That son of his should be just a little more like him.

SANDRA

Why you always picking on Derek?

ANN

I'm not picking on him. It's just that...

SANDRA

Just that what?

ANN

Well... I mean... Look how long he's going out with you and up to now he hasn't said a thing to me about his intentions. His father would never have done such a thing.

SANDRA

Times have changed, Mommy.

5

ANN

Well I think it's high time he let me know what he's about.

SANDRA

It's not you he's dating, you know.

ANN

What he said to you then? You're not getting any younger, you know. It's time you start to think about getting a husband. I hope Derek isn't just blocking traffic.

SANDRA

To tell you the truth, Mommy, we're not planning to get married.

ANN

What? I couldn't be hearing you right. No sensible girl is going to be running here and there with a man every minute, unless she planning to marry him.

SANDRA

Marriage isn't everything.

ANN

Every sensible woman wants to get married. What you want to be, an ole maid?

SANDRA

I'm surely not going to be any ole maid either.

ANN

Well, what you think is going to happen to you if you fool around now? You're not going to be young all your life.

SANDRA

You may as well start getting accustomed to the idea, Mommy. When Derek finishes university we're going to rent a house and just live together.

ANN

You mustn't joke about serious things like that you know, girl.

SANDRA

But I'm dead serious.

ANN

Dead serious?

SANDRA

Dead serious.

ANN

(Getting up)

Dead crazy, you mean.

(Sandra lights a cigarette)

ANN

I tired tell you I don't want you smoking no cigarette in my house.

SANDRA

Okay, Mommy.

ANN

All this university education is corrupting the minds of you young people. How can you even think of such a thing? I told your father, "Andrew, I'm not in favor of sending Sandra to any university," and he wouldn't listen to me.

7

ANN (Continued)

Now look what happen. Just look what you have come to.

SANDRA

You're making it sound as if I'm some sort of a criminal. Me and Derek love each other, and that's the only thing that's going to keep us together. Not repeating a couple of stupid vows and signing a piece of paper.

ANN

So when he pick up and leave you, what you're going to do then? Who is going to work for you?

SANDRA

I'm an educated woman, Mommy. I don't need a man to work for me.

ANN

But you don't have any hold over him. He could fool around with any other woman he wants to.

SANDRA

I don't see the marriage vows stopping any of these married men today from fooling around. And some of the women too. Besides, if he is going to be free to fool around, then so am I.

ANN

You mean to tell me this is all the ambition you have, Sandra? All the ambition you have? To go and live in sin with a man?

SANDRA

(Coming towards her)

Don't be upset, Mommy. It hasn't happened as yet and it's still a long way off. And there's something else I have to tell you too.

ANN

Well if it's anything like this I don't want to hear it.

(Sandra shrugs)

ANN

What is it?

SANDRA

Nothing serious. I'll tell you some other time. When you're not so upset.

ANN

Upset? Upset you call it? What has happened to all you've learned about the work of God, Sandra? Dear Jesus, what is the world coming to today? I hope you're still a virtuous young lady.

SANDRA

I'm 23 years old, Mommy!

ANN

So what? When I got married I was 24, and still as fresh as a blossom. Ask your father.

SANDRA

For heaven's sake, Mommy...

(She breaks off and clutches her middle)

9

SANDRA (Continued)

Oh God!

(She rushes over and collapses on the couch)

ANN

Sandra! What's wrong, child? What's the matter with you?

SANDRA

(Hardly able to talk)

Nothing. Just a cutting in my belly.

ANN

This thing is getting serious.

(She starts moving off)

Let me call...

SANDRA

(Reaching out and grabbing her)
I'll be okay in a little while. It's nothing.

ANN

Don't give me...

(The doorbell cuts her off)

I'll see who it is.

(Before she reaches the door, it is pushed open and Derek walks in)

DEREK

Hello, Mrs. Forgerty.

ANN

Oh, hello, Derek.

DEREK

How's life?

ANN

Not as good as you, my son. The pressure has been troubling me and you know I always suffer from dizziness.

DEREK

I thought you had gotten over the dizzy spells long ago.

ANN

Not at all. I still get them off and on.

DEREK

Anyway, you're looking as fit as a fiddle to me.

(He sees Sandra on couch)

Hey, Sandra.

SANDRA

(Still a bit feeble)
Hi, Derek.

DEREK

What's the matter with you?

(He crosses from Ann to Sandra)

You're sick or something?

SANDRA

Just a pain in my belly.

ANN

I'm sure something is wrong with her. I was just going to call the doctor.

SANDRA

(Sitting up. To Derek)

Don't worry with Mommy, eh.

(To Ann)

I told you I was going to see the doctor, didn't I? It doesn't make sense to call him now.

DEREK

What's there to eat? I'm hungry as a dog.

SANDRA

What have you been up to?

DEREK

Been working out some new dance steps with the group.

SANDRA

I'll go see what's in the kitchen.

ANN

You sit down and relax, Sandra. I'll rustle up something.

(She leaves)

DEREK

(Getting closer to Sandra)

So what's going on?

SANDRA

Things don't look so good.

DEREK

What is that supposed to mean?

SANDRA

I think I'm pregnant.

DEREK

That's bad news. I was hoping you'd see your period by now. Maybe it will still come.

SANDRA

Well. It's two long months now. And I'm never late. Plus I've been vomiting and just feeling sick all the time.

DEREK

That is bad news. Does your mother suspect anything?

SANDRA

I don't think so. But I can't keep it from her much longer. I've been sick and she's threatening to call the doctor. I don't know how to tell her.

DEREK

Maybe that's not a bad idea.

DEREK (Continued)

(Turning to Sandra)

Calling the doctor I mean. Why don't you get the doctor to give you some tablets or something and take care of it? Then you wouldn't have to tell anybody anything.

SANDRA

I've thought of that, Derek. But I can't.

DEREK

Oh come on, Sandra, half the girls in town...

SANDRA

That is surely no reason why I should!

DEREK

(Sarcastically)

Well... Maybe you have some better ideas.

SANDRA

Why don't I just have the child?

DEREK

Don't be ridiculous.

SANDRA

I'm not being ridiculous. I'm serious. Why don't I just have the child?

DEREK

Look Sandra. We have agreed that marriage is out of the question. Apart from that I'm still at school. The time isn't right for any of that crap.

14

SANDRA

Who said anything about getting married? I'll have the baby, and by the time you finish university and we start living together. Our family will be well on its way.

DEREK

You realise what you're saying?

SANDRA

Of course it's going to create a big scandal at first, and there'll be hassles with people like Mother, but it will all die down. Besides, I do want the baby.

DEREK

(Chuckles a bit)

Sounds interesting.

(Thoughtfully)

I'm beginning to like the idea.

(Laughing outright)

Just imagine me being a papa.

(They both laugh and embrace each other)

SANDRA

You can afford to laugh. I'm the one who's pregnant.

(Ann has entered in time to hear the last of this. They realise she is in the room when the tray she is carrying crashes to the floor)

15

ANN

Pregnant! Sandra you pregnant? Oh my God, what is this for me at all? Lord Jesus what is this for me?

SANDRA

Don't work up yourself like that, Mommy.

(Picking things up)

ANN

Who did this to you?

SANDRA

Oh Mommy, who else could it be?

(She takes tray to sideboard)

DEREK

That's a good question.

ANN

How could you do such a thing Derek? After all the confidence we had in you these five years?

SANDRA

Please, Mommy...

ANN

You be quiet. I should have put my foot down on your nonsense long ago.

SANDRA

Well, it's too late to start now, Mommy. Just relax.

ANN

Don't you have any shame girl? Think of what people are going to say. Our good name will be dragging in the gutters.

SANDRA

Oh please...

ANN

That might mean nothing to you, but think of me and your father.

SANDRA

There's nothing disgraceful about being pregnant, Mommy.

ANN

You have the nerves to watch me in my face and talk about no disgrace? Well, something has to be done about it.

SANDRA

Please, Mommy, just leave...

ANN

The only thing that can save us now is for both of you to get married before the news gets around.

(To Derek)
I hope you know this means you will have to marry Sandra?

DEREK

Just leave it to us, Mrs. Forgerty. We'll see to it that everything works out fine.

(James enters from the street immediately followed by Andrew)

JAMES

Hello my dear, Ann. How're you doing?

JAMES (Continued)

(Examining her)

By God, you look like a million.

ANN

Oh, Mr. Wellington, it's so nice to see you. You and Andrew are just in time to hear the good news.

ANDREW

What good news?

ANN

Well...

JAMES

Come on. Out with it, out with it.

ANN

Sandra and Derek are going to get married.

JAMES

Married!

ANDREW

Married?

JAMES

How the devil I haven't heard anything about this 'till now?

ANN

They just decided suddenly. Tonight. Just now.

JAMES

I expected they would get married eventually and that it would be a grand occasion. But the damn boy is still...wait a minute. The girl in trouble or something?

ANN

Shh, not so loud. You know how these young people blood hot.

JAMES

(Turning to Derek and. Sandra)

How in heavens the two of you could allow such a thing to happen?

DEREK

The usual way, Daddy. The usual way.

(Andrew chuckles)

JAMES

(Slightly annoyed)

This is no time for foolishness. We have to discuss the matter seriously.

ANN

One thing I know, the wedding will have to be soon to prevent any scandal.

JAMES

But of course.

DEREK

There isn't going to be any wedding.

19

ANN

But…but, there has to be!

ANDREW

Ann, Ann.

JAMES

Listen boy, you can't just walk into the home of a decent family like this, abuse their daughter and walk out as if nothing happen.

SANDRA

He hasn't abused me. I'm just as much responsible as he is. If not more so.

ANN

Sandra!

JAMES

That's beside the point. He still can't run out on you now.

SANDRA

What's the matter with all of you? He isn't running out on me. I'm going to have the baby, and when he's finished school we're going to live together.

ANDREW

Just like that?

JAMES

Young people today don't understand life.

ANDREW

If both of you plan to live together and raise a family, why not just get married and done?

DEREK

Because marriage is outdated and becoming more and more meaningless. We don't want any part of it.

ANN

But the word of the Lord…

ANDREW

Ann…Ann! Just go get us something to drink please.

ANN

That's the trouble with you, Andrew. You never want to hear anything about the word of God.

(To James)

That's the whole trouble with him.

JAMES

I'm quite sure, my dear. A cold beer will do me fine.

(Still annoyed she turns to go. When she has made a few steps Andrew speaks)

ANDREW

Bring one for me too.

ANN

(Stopping but not looking around)

What about the rest of you?

SANDRA

Nothing for me, thank you.

DEREK

Nothing for me either.

ANN

(She leaves)

ANDREW

Look, I know many marriages aren't perfect. Nothing is perfect.

DEREK

We know that too, but what about the marriage vows? Do they? They expect every marriage to be perfect. They ask you to pledge to stick with each other for better for worse; to love, honor and respect each other forever. How could any honest sensible person make such a promise not knowing what's going to happen in five years, five months, five weeks? If two people should discover they're not compatible any more, what should they do? Live in misery for the rest of their lives as the vows ask or separate in peace and try again? The thing is just ridiculous!

ANDREW

Fair enough. But in that event what is going to...

JAMES

(Crossing in front of Andrew and coming closer to Sandra and Derek)

These children don't know what they're talking about.

(To Sandra)

Do you realise that this boy of mine will be able to take off and leave you anytime?

SANDRA

Nobody ever takes off and leaves a good thing. Besides, look how many husbands leave their wives, and wives leave their husbands. Marriage doesn't guarantee that all is going to go well. If our relationship is good, we'll find a way to work things out. If it isn't then all the marriage vows in the world wouldn't help.

JAMES

You don't realise all that's involved. What's going to happen to the children?

(Ann comes in with beers)

SANDRA

They'll be the same as any other children.

ANN

They'll be bastards.

JAMES

Do you realise that unless you are married the law offers little or no protection for you or for the child you're going to have?

SANDRA

That's a terrible shame. But nonetheless, what protection does the law give to children in a family where the parents are just staying together 'for the sake of the children'. What protection do children have from seeing their mother cry over and over again, because their father is out running around with some one of his…whores?

ANN

Sandra! Watch your language.

SANDRA

(Brushing her aside with a wave of her hand)

If Derek and I are any kind of decent human beings, we'll make every effort to see that our children are adequately looked after without the force of the law, or the dubious merits of a marriage ceremony.

JAMES

That might sound good in theory, but what makes you think it can work?

DEREK

Marriage is a gamble, life is a gamble. Why should living together be any different? All we're saying is that a meaningful relationship has nothing to do with marriage vows or license.

JAMES

Listen to me. This is a serious situation. Sandra is in trouble and going to live in sin is surely not the best solution to the problem.

ANN

Exactly!

JAMES

Derek, do you...

DEREK

Listen Daddy, I'm tired and hungry and I don't want to argue about it anymore.

DEREK (Continued)

Sandra and I are going out for a while so I can have something to eat and talk things over.

(They start to leave)

ANN

(Moving towards them)

You're not going anywhere, Sandra.

ANDREW

(Blocking her)

Leave them alone, Ann.

(They exit)

ANN

That's the whole problem with you, Andrew. You spoiled her. You've always spoiled her. And look what happens now. She's going to disgrace the whole family. If you had listened to me and made her go to church...

ANDREW

Did going to church prevent you from becoming pregnant?

ANN

There's no need to bring up that now. Besides as soon as we realised our mistake, we got married and cleared it up.

ANDREW

Well I'm certainly not going to force them to get married.

25

ANN

We can't let them go through with it. Sandra having a bastard and living in sin. We can't let that happen, Andrew.

JAMES

I quite agree with you, Ann. Something has got to be done.

ANDREW

They're two sensible people. Just leave them to themselves and I'm sure things will work themselves out.

JAMES

When you leave things to work themselves out, they never work out right. I'm a man who believes in making things work right.

ANN

So what we going to do then?

JAMES

Don't worry about it. Don't worry about it one little bit.

(He comes between them and rests his hand on one shoulder of each)

I'll take care of everything in a weak or so when I get back from Guyana, I'll see that everything is organized. After all, never let it be said that I, James Llewellyn Wellington, couldn't take care of a simple situation like this.

BLACKOUT

ACT I

SCENE 2

(The back veranda of Mr. Wellington's house. Mid-morning)

(When the scene opens, Molly is relaxing in the big chair. When she hears James shouting from inside, she jumps up and straightens herself, knocking over a bottle of beer she is drinking)

JAMES

(From inside)

Anybody home? Derek? Molly?

(He enters just as Molly has scrambled to her feet. He is dressed in suit and tie and carries a briefcase)

MOLLY

Oh is you, sah. You frighten me. Me no me expect you so early.

JAMES

I can see that. You don't expect me so you lie down and cock up in my chair, eh?

MOLLY

Oh no, sah!

JAMES

What's been happening since I've been away?

MOLLY

Not'ing at all, sah.

JAMES

Where's Derek?

MOLLY

He left early and said he wouldn't be back till late. But me glad fuh see you, sah. You look nice.

JAMES

This is the only place in the world I know where people expect to get money and don't work for it.

MOLLY

Wha' you saying, sah?

JAMES

You do any work for the day, Molly?

MOLLY

Of course, sah, plenty, plenty.

JAMES

You had better be right, or that beer comes out your pay at the end of the week.

(Joe enters carrying a suitcase. He has come around to the back so he walks on stage from in the audience)

JOE

Where to put this, sah?

JAMES

Leave it any place there. Molly will take it in. The wife and family keeping okay?

JOE

Everybody alright, sah. An dem did tell me fu tell you howdy. De Madam going to de ground today so she will bring down some provisions for you.

JAMES

Good. Tell them I say howdy too.

(Turns to go)

JOE

(Clearing his throat to remind James that he has not been paid)
Er, er…sah?

JAMES

Oh, I forgot that.

(Feels his pockets)

Check me out in the office tomorrow, Joe, and we'll straighten that out.

JOE

You no have nothing…

JAMES

Tomorrow!

JOE

Right-o, sah, me'll see you then.

(They both turn to go. Joe hesitates until James is inside, then turns back)

So what's going on, Molly?

MOLLY
Me just a tek it easy, boy.

JOE
You looking well sweet and nice.

(He tries to touch her)

MOLLY
No get fresh wid me eh, boy!

JOE
Wha' wrong wid you tall? You mean me can't touch you no more?

MOLLY
Why you no go touch you wife?

JOE
But if me touch me wife alone all de time me soon get fed-up.

MOLLY
Well, no come touch me.

JOE
You well up pan you high hoss today. No tell me dat is de boss touching you up now.

MOLLY
A wha' you a say tall?

JOE
Me know he sharp lek a razor blade.

MOLLY

Well, he better no come play no fool wid me either.
Me gat me man.

JOE

So dat is why you getting on so these days. You nar
bother wid me at all at all.

MOLLY

You a somebody fu badder wid?

JOE

You no even self gee me the latest flash.

MOLLY

Me no know wha' you a talk bout.

JOE

No tell me you no hear how Derek breed off Mr.
Forgerty daughter?

MOLLY

A wha' you a say tall? Me no hear a thing.

JOE

A joke you a gee.

MOLLY

Me nar joke, me no hear nuttn.

JOE

Well, it all over town, gel.

31

MOLLY

When you nose right in a de pot you never could smell, for true. Anyway de two of them could just get married and done. Dem a friend long enough.

JOE

Dat a de trouble gel. Derek say he nar get married.

MOLLY

So you mean he jus' me a fool off de poor gel all this time? Ah you man really worthless for true, sah.

JOE

You no begin to hear nothing yet.

MOLLY

Well me a listen.

JOE

Dis is just between you and me, you know.

MOLLY

You know me wouldn't even tell me own mother, man.

JOE

Mark you, no go say me say.

JOE

Gel, dem gat big bacchanal down a de Forgerty house de other night. Mrs. Forgerty collar up Derek and shake he out and ask he wha' he intend to do 'bout she daughter.

MOLLY

For true, for true?

JOE

Me nar lie you, de woman get bad. She rant and rave and cuss, but all de carry on she carry on, Derek still decide he no in a nothing wid no wedding.

MOLLY

A wha' me a hear ya tall!

JOE

Wait man, me a tell you how it go. Things get so bad, dem have to send for de big boss.

MOLLY

Mr. Wellington?

JOE

Mr. James Llewellyn Wellington himself.

MOLLY

Me a tell you.

JOE

And from the time de big boss hit de scene, everything cool. He tell Derek he have to come better than that.

MOLLY

De boss no easy for true.

JOE

You telling me. But me hear just tidday self that Derek still a say he no in a nuttn wid no marriding.

MOLLY

So wha' a go happen?

JOE

Derek feel that he tough, but he will soon see who tough. Anyway gel, me have to mek a fast trip to the airport, so me rushing off now.

MOLLY

But you no done tell me how de story go.

JOE

Me can't stop now. So why you don't let me pick you up later and we could talk about it?

MOLLY

A smart you a play?

JOE

No, gel, wha' you a go on wid? A we could discuss de whole ting later and me will gee you all de details.

MOLLY

Well...well, alright then. Me see you later.

JOE

Keep you mouth shut now.

MOLLY

No worry 'bout that man. Take it easy.

(He leaves. She immediately goes to the phone and dials)

Bella, ah you dat? Me got one bone fu pick wid you. How come you no gee me de latest gist? Yes...dat a what me a talk 'bout. Gel, me no hear a thing meself till today. What a thing pan God earth for true?

MOLLY (Continued)

Mrs. Forgerty pickney breed arf! Me agree wid you gel, it serve she just right. Yes, yes, you right wid dat. De 'ole gel so science wid she self, she no even does tell neaga howdy. Derek should never piss pan she. A so me hear gel! Dardy-oh, me never nutn lek dis since me bam...

(She laughs loudly)

Look, it sound lek de mister coming, so me have to go. But a we got to pound story pan dis later. See you.

(James reappears. He has changed his clothes and is looking fresh and relaxed)

JAMES

I thought I heard Joe out here still.

MOLLY

He just left, sah.

JAMES

He wanted something?

MOLLY

He was trying to get fresh wid me, sah, so I had to put him in his place.

JAMES

Well, that's the two of you business. Go bring me a beer or something.

(As she passes him he slaps her on the rear)

You have a good little ass here, you know.

35

MOLLY

You better behave you self, eh.

(She exits. James sits down and is leafing through his newspaper, when Molly reappears)

A nice young lady out there to see you, sah.

JAMES

Who is it?

MOLLY

I don't know she name, sah, but is de same one you had last week.

JAMES

Show her in…who ever the devil it may be.

CAROL

(Carol enters from house. She is about 28 and nicely dressed)

I'm in already, Romeo.

JAMES

(Jumping up)

Oh, Carol, it's you! How're you doing honey bunch? Come on over here let me have a look at you.

(He looks her over)

Man, you're looking good enough for a king.

CAROL

You really think so?

JAMES

Bet your life I do.

(He hugs her and tries to kiss her, but she stiffens as Molly is looking at all this with eager eyes. James frowns at her)

What are you hanging around for?

MOLLY

Ar...er...

JAMES

Never mind. Take the rest of the day off.

MOLLY

But what about the beer, sah?

JAMES

Just disappear, Molly.

(She exits)

Make sure you're early tomorrow.

(He leads Carol over to one of the chairs, pulls up one close to her and sits on it)

CAROL

Why did you send her away?

JAMES

(Putting his hand around her in an intimate way)

Well, why do you think?

CAROL

(Resisting him)

I can't stay very long.

JAMES

It's been a whole long week since I saw you last.

CAROL

That's true, but I just dropped in for a few minutes. I heard on the radio you had a successful trip and was back early, so I just passed to see how you were.

JAMES

Well, what's the big hurry?

CAROL

I've got so many things to do. First of all, I have to pick up a dress at the seamstress and take it to show Sandra. And then...

JAMES

That can't prevent you from spending a little time with me.

CAROL

Tonight, James. Then you can take me to Vue Pointe and we can have a real swing.

JAMES

Tonight is a long way off. Up to now you haven't even kissed me.

(She puts her arms around his neck and is about to kiss him when Ann calls from inside)

ANN

Mr. Wellington, Mr. Wellington dear!

(She enters)

JAMES

(James grimaces)

Are you...

(Ann stops dead as she sees them in each other's arms)

JAMES

(The grimace on James' face changes into a smile)

Oh Ann, how nice to see you.

ANN

I hope I'm not interrupting anything. I didn't realise you were busy.

CAROL

It's alright, I was just leaving. Don't forget tonight, dear.

JAMES

Not at all. Take it easy now.

(She exits)

ANN

Who is that girl?

JAMES

You don't know her?

39

ANN

No.

JAMES

Of course you do. That's one of the new teachers from Trinidad. Carol Summersdale. She's Sandra's friend.

ANN

Oh, so that's her. I hear Sandra speaking about her all the time but I've never met her. Well, she certainly hasn't wasted any time.

JAMES

You can say that again.

ANN

And you. You're just as bad a wolf as they say.

JAMES

You better watch out that this bad wolf doesn't eat you up. You're a fine looking woman, you know.

ANN

You ought to be ashamed of yourself, Mr. Wellington. Fooling around with a little girl like that. She could almost be your daughter.

JAMES

Ann my dear, instead of scolding me, why don't you help me to correct my wrong doings.

ANN

Would, would you like me to pray with you?

JAMES

Oh no.

ANN

Well, how can I help you then?

JAMES

By letting me fool around with you instead.

ANN

You wouldn't dare!

JAMES

(Laughing)

Oh no, no, no. Of course not. I'm only pulling your leg.

(He shows her to a chair and they both sit)

Well, did you want to see me for something special?

ANN

Er…yes, yes. About the wedding.

JAMES

Oh yes, of course. I'm looking after it. Don't worry.

ANN

I am a bit worried. Nobody has said a thing to me and people are starting to talk. Plus the church…

JAMES

Don't worry about it. Now that I'm back everything will be looked after.

41

ANN

I know that you would take care of things. Andrew wouldn't lift a finger.

JAMES

I'm sure he's only busy with his work.

ANN

You don't know Andrew. Oh well.

(Pause)

But you're still quite a young man yourself. Why don't you get married again?

JAMES

Well, my dear Dorothy's memory, bless her, is still very near and dear to me. So I imagine it would be quite some time before I can even think of such things.

ANN

It's over a year now since she passed away, isn't it?

JAMES

Yes, but I still think that's too soon.

ANN

You're such a considerate man. Giving her due honor and respect even in the grave. Andrew would never do such a thing for me.

JAMES

Oh I'm quite sure he would.

ANN

You don't understand. Nobody understands.

(She turns away. He suddenly reaches out, grabs her and kisses her. For a brief moment, her hand reaches up as if she is going to embrace him. Then she pulls away and jumps up)

Don't do that. If the church should…

JAMES

(Getting up right after her)

The church, the church, the church! Everything is the church. We have to give vent to our feelings, Ann.

(He tries to embrace her)

ANN

No. Wait! I've never done anything like this before.

JAMES

Of course you haven't.

(Under his breath)

It's always the first time.

(Normal voice)

Listen Ann, we are only human. The Lord will under-stand and forgive.

(He embraces her again. This time she allows herself to be embraced. Just as he is about to kiss her, she pulls away her head)

ANN

People might pass and see us.

43

JAMES
What people? There're no people around.

ANN
(Pointing to the audience)

Who are those?

JAMES
Those don't matter. They don't know who we are.

ANN
Are you sure?

JAMES
Of course I'm sure. Besides they're minding their own business.

(They embrace and kiss. While they are still holding each other, James eases her over to the big chair, inch by inch. Just as they have both slipped onto the chair, James lying on Ann, Derek is heard off stage)

DEREK
Dad! Daddy! Are you outside?

(Both James and Ann jump to a sitting position. James quickly forces Ann to stand up. When Derek enters, James is lying in the chair with one hand gripping an arm of the bewildered Ann, who is standing over him James lets off a groan, looks up and speaks to Ann in a feeble voice)

JAMES
I think I'll be alright now, Ann. If you just step inside and get me two aspirins I'll be able to manage.

ANN

(Badly shaken)

Er...yes, yes, Mr. Wellington.

JAMES

Oh Derek, It's you?

DEREK

What on earth...

JAMES

My trip must have worn me out more than I expected. If it wasn't for Ann, I might have passed right
out.

(Ann, who has started for the door very unsteadily,
swoons. Derek catches her before she hits the
ground)

DEREK

This passing out business seems to be catching.
Help me get her over to the chair.

(They both lift her over to the chair)

What's this? Some kind of fainting epidemic or something?

JAMES

This looks serious. I can't understand it. If she wasn't
here I might have fallen and injured myself. And now
look at her.

DEREK

I'm looking. You want me to call the doctor?

JAMES

No, no. It's not that serious.

DEREK

How you know?

JAMES

It can't be anything serious.

DEREK

What have you been doing to the poor woman, Dad?

JAMES

What do you mean, 'What have I been doing to the woman?' Nothing! We were just there talking, then all of a sudden I almost passed out. Well don't look at me that way. You think I'd lie to you.

ANN

What happened? Where am I?

JAMES

(Moving towards her)

Easy now, Ann, easy.

(He changes his mind)

You better look after her.

DEREK

Okay, Mrs. Forgerty, there's nothing to worry about. You must have had one of your spells. I'll take you inside and get you something to drink and put you to lay down so you can rest for awhile.

DEREK (Continued)

(He puts one of her arms over his shoulder and takes her inside)

JAMES

What the hell is this for me at all? When is not one damn thing is the next.

(Carol enters from back yard)

CAROL

You're still here, darling? Good. I was hoping you hadn't taken off on one of your many little missions.

JAMES

Carol, I thought…

CAROL

Yes, but I changed my mind. Decided to spend some time with you after all.

(She gives him a peck on the cheek)

Well, aren't you glad?

JAMES

Oh yes, of course, of course. Only I'm so busy right now. I've got some business to talk over with Derek.

CAROL

I thought Derek was out.

JAMES

He got back just a few minutes ago. So while we're here together for a change, I might as well grab the chance to talk over things with him.

47

CAROL

That's okay. Go right ahead and talk. I'll just slip into the kitchen and cook you both some curry chicken. How's that? There should still be roti skins in the freezer from last time.

(Derek enters)

JAMES

Oh no, no. I couldn't let you do that. Why don't you drop over and see Sandra as planned, and I'll pick you up later and take you to Vue Pointe for dinner.

DEREK

Did I hear roti?

CAROL

(Turning to Derek whose presence was not noticed until now)

I think your father is trying to get rid of me. Okay, Derek, I'll cook just enough curry chicken and roti for you.

DEREK

That's just fine with me, baby.

JAMES

Okay, okay. Make it. But I don't think you should go through all that trouble.

CAROL

No trouble at all.

(She exits)

JAMES

I hope you realise what you might be getting me into.

DEREK

Me?

JAMES

What you think she's going to think when she sees Ann here?

DEREK

What's there for her to think?

JAMES

You know women.

DEREK

Don't worry about it, Dad. Besides, if she doesn't go into your bedroom, she'll probably not see Ann at all.

JAMES

Into my bedroom?

DEREK

Well, that's where the closest bed was.

JAMES

She got to be moved.

(He hurries off)

DEREK

No Dad, wait.

(He hurries after James)

CAROL

(She enters with two bottles of beer in her hands)

These should help to keep you two boys...James! Derek!

JAMES

(From inside)

We're coming.

CAROL

(She places beer on table)

I brought you two some beer. It's on the table.

(She turns to go but sees James' suitcase)

I'd better take this in and unpack it when I get a chance.

(She exits)

DEREK

(He enters, bringing James with him)

What's the matter with you? You can't go and rouse her now. You'll just upset the woman all over again.

JAMES

Okay, okay. You've made your point.

DEREK

(Grabbing a beer)

Carol brought us some beer.

(Gives one to James)

JAMES

Good. I could use a drink.

(Takes a long drag)

I didn't even get a chance to compliment you on your performance the other night.

DEREK

What performance?

JAMES

The way you handled the little situation over by the Forgerty's. Evading the issue of marriage. You know what I mean. Cornered but playing for time. Temporizing like a true diplomat. Brilliant. But there's nothing to worry about. Your Dad will get you out of this little jam.

DEREK

I don't think I quite read you, Dad.

JAMES

We both know you can't afford to get married now. You've got your studies to think about first.

DEREK

I have no intention of getting married.

JAMES

Exactly. So I'll arrange to have Dr. Walcheck take care of the girl. You know what I mean.

(Derek attempts to speak but is cut off)

51

JAMES

Of course the mother is going to be a little upset about this. But I'll make her see that it's the best thing for the time being. After you get out of school, you could get married then.

DEREK

Listen, Dad, your friend Dr. Walcheck isn't going to take care of anything.

JAMES

(Already on his way to the phone)

I'll just get on the phone…now wait a minute! What did you say?

DEREK

You heard me. I said your friend Dr. Walcheck isn't going to take care of anything.

JAMES

Now let me make sure I get this clear. The girl is with child?

DEREK

Urn-huh.

JAMES

She's going to keep the child?

DEREK

Urn-huh.

JAMES

And you're not going to marry her?

DEREK
Right.

JAMES
You're not going to tell me that you were really serious about all the shit you were shooting the other night?

DEREK
You know, Dad, you're right again. Go to the head of the class.

JAMES
Come on Derek. You have to have more sense than that. You know you can't do such a thing. Look, if you and Sandra want to have a child, fine. It's about time I had some grandchildren anyway. True you're young and still in university and all that, but there's nothing wrong with settling down while you're young. I'd hardly turned twenty when I married your mother myself. We'll have a big wedding and settle everything.

DEREK
A big wedding, a big party, a big spree. The answer to all your problems. The best solution to every pregnancy.

JAMES
What have you got against marriage anyway?

DEREK
I'm tired of going over that.

JAMES

And what about Sandra? What does she feel?

DEREK

You know she feels the same way about it as I do.

JAMES

If you believe that, then you're an even bigger fool than I thought. There's no such thing on earth as a woman who doesn't want to get married.

DEREK

We'll see.

JAMES

Listen son. The Forgerty's are a decent and respectable family. You can't expect Sandra to go an have a bastard like some... common country girl?

DEREK

You see how you think? It's all well and good for some 'common country girl' to have a bastard child, which she cannot afford. But no such disgraceful behavior from the daughter of a decent respectable family! I suppose it is decent and respectable to throw away the child?

JAMES

That's beside the point.

DEREK

No it isn't.

JAMES

Arguing isn't going to get us anywhere. Do me a favor and marry the girl.

54

JAMES (Continued)

Elections are next year and a scandal like this could be harmful to me. And, after all, what's harmful to me is also harmful to you.

DEREK

You really think people worry about the private lives of you politicians? If they did, which one of you would ever stand a chance of getting elected to office?

JAMES

I agree that some of these young fellows don't have any discretion. But give them a chance, they'll see.

DEREK

They're not going to see a thing. The people have always been aware of the way you older guys carry on. You think they're stupid?

JAMES

That might be so. But it's not what you do, it's how you do it. If people think you're trying to be discrete they will look away. On the other hand, if you're too brazen…

DEREK

Tell you what, Dad you concern yourself with what you do and how you do it in office. That is what is going to determine whether or not you get back in power. Not how I choose to live my life.

CAROL

(Rushing in and confronting James)

55

CAROL (Continued)

So that's what it is, eh? That is why you didn't want me around!

JAMES

Oh, Christ! Let me explain…

CAROL

I don't want to hear anything. I saw her. It's not anybody tell me this time. And if I didn't take in your suitcase to unpack it I would never have known.

(He tries to put his arms around her. She screams)

Don't touch me. I've had more shit from you than I'm prepared to take and I'm damn sick and tired of it.

(She storms off)

JAMES

Women! Goddam women! Why the hell can't anything go right with them?

DEREK

Quite a hot mama that one. If you're so anxious for a wedding, why don't you marry her?

JAMES

Forget about her. Forget the hell about her and let's get back to our affairs.

DEREK

It's a waste of time, Dad. I'm just not going to get married.

56

JAMES

Don't tell me it's a waste of time. I say you marry the girl and that's final.

DEREK

Relax, Dad. You're losing your cool.

JAMES

The amount of things you've put me through would make the North Pole lose its cool. But not any more, Derek. Not one damn.

DEREK

What are you working up yourself so for? Listen, Daddy, try and understand…

JAMES

How long do you expect me to go on trying to understand? When you finally decided to go to university, I told you study law, study political science, study medicine, something useful. No, you want to study sociology. Alright, I agree. I send you to Canada. Instead of going up there, keeping your tail quiet and learning your lessons, what you do? You go get yourself mixed up with that Rosie Douglas fellow and those other hooligans and burn the people's university down. All of that I take. And now you want to embarrass and humiliate me again? Well not this time my friend. Not this time.

DEREK

There're some things that people like you with your colonial mentalities will never be able to understand.

JAMES
I don't want to hear any of that shit. Colonial mentality, or colonial mentality not, around here what I say still carries.

DEREK
What are you trying to do? Force me to get married or something?

JAMES
All I'm saying is to make up your mind what you're doing by tonight. And if you can't see things my way, then take your belongings and find some place else to go. Is my way or de highway.

(Derek shrugs. James starts walking off then swings back)

And you might as well forget about me paying the rest of your way through school.

(He storms off)

DEREK

(Calling out to him)

Daddy!

(The door slams)

Shit! What the hell's a man to do?

(Sandra enters from garden)

SANDRA
Derek, what was that about? All the shouting?

DEREK

Just a quarrel with the old man.

SANDRA

Well, I gathered that much…

DEREK

Then why the hell are you asking me stupid questions?

SANDRA

Hey, I'm not that old man you know. Don't go lashing out at me.

(Silence. She walks over to him)

Come on Derek, snap out of it.

(She tries to tickle him. He pushes her away)

DEREK

I'm just not in the mood for playing around, Sandra.

SANDRA

Well, tell me what happened then.

(He sits on one of the chairs. She moves a few steps towards him)

Well?

DEREK

I just got kicked out of the house and my tuition fees have been cut off.

SANDRA

Why would James want to do a thing like that?

59

DEREK

He's trying to muscle me into getting married.

SANDRA

Derek?

(She rests her right hand lovingly on his right shoulder, moves slowly around the chair and sits down on his left knee with her arm over his shoulder)

Wouldn't it be simpler it we just get married?

DEREK

(Pushing her off and jumping up in one motion)

No! That's absolutely out of the question.

SANDRA

(Offended)

Surely Derek, there's no need for you to get fanatical about it. Mother is so upset about the whole thing, that if we don't get married I'm sure she's going to lose her mind. And now this thing with your father. You know how pig-headed he is.

DEREK

That's the whole point. You don't expect me to have the old man pushing me around and telling me how to live my life?

SANDRA

But it all seems such a great big pointless struggle.

DEREK

That's life.

(Silence)

SANDRA

Derek?

(She walks slowly over to him and puts both arms around his neck)

Do you love me?

DEREK

Of course I do.

SANDRA

Well why are you so against marrying me? Am I not good enough to be your legal wife?

(He laughs. She withdraws her arms)

What's so funny?

DEREK

I'm just laughing about something Dad said about every woman wanting to get married. Look Sandra, we have plenty of time to quarrel. Right now, we should be sticking together.

SANDRA

You still haven't answered me.

(Pause)

Well, are you going to marry me?

DEREK

No, I'm not.

61

SANDRA

Oh, really? So that's how it is?

(She turns quickly and starts to hurry off. He runs and grabs her)

DEREK

Come on, Sandra. You know I'm head over heels in love with you. How could I ever think of marrying you and have marriage turn you into a fat and peevish old lady within a few years?

SANDRA

(Laughing in spite of herself)

Oh, Derek, you're such a scream.

(She embraces him. They laugh and kiss)

DEREK

Nothing like a good bit of loving to take a man's mind off his troubles. But I'm afraid I'm still in the same rut.

(He plops down in one of the chairs)

Well, I guess I'll just have to find myself a permanent job and forget about school for the time being.

SANDRA

No Derek. That will never do. We're in this together. And with you working part time and me working all year round, we should be able to manage the fees.

DEREK

(He pulls her into his lap and kisses her)

DEREK (Continued)

You know, if I ever decide to get married, you're the
first on my list. Come help me pack.

(He picks her up in his arms and walks out with her)

(The lights fade slowly until the stage is quite dimly lit.
Then Ann enters)

ANN

Derek? Mr....Mr. Wellington? Nobody seems to be
here. Well, look what a mess I nearly get myself in.

(She crosses herself)

Never me again!

BLACKOUT

63

ACT II

(The set is the same as Act I, Scene 1. It is late afternoon. When the lights come up the stage is empty. The front door opens and Andrew walks on with his briefcase. He rubs his eyes. Sandra shouts from the bedroom.)

SANDRA

Is that you, Dad?

ANDREW

Yes.

SANDRA

(Entering)

Only now you coming from work or you were out liming?

ANDREW

Straight from work. And I'm dead beat.

SANDRA

(Taking briefcase)

Here let me take this in for you.

(From inside)

You want your slippers, Dad?

ANDREW

Thanks.

(He goes over to the liquor cabinet and pours himself a drink, then relaxes in the couch)

SANDRA

(Returning)

Why the long hours?

ANDREW

I was working on a speech for James and that held me.

(He rubs his eye)

SANDRA

Something in your eye?

ANDREW

It's been bothering me all afternoon. As if sand or something is in it.

SANDRA

Let me see.

(She looks into the eye)

I don't see anything. Hold on.

(She blows into the eye)

How's that?

ANDREW

It's so sore that I don't even know.

SANDRA

Come again.

(She blows again)

ANDREW

Okay, let that do. I'll see in a while if it's any better. How was your day?

Act II

SANDRA
So, so.

ANDREW
Problems?

SANDRA
Well, yes!

ANDREW
What new developments?

SANDRA
None that I know of, but I'm expecting Carol to stop by any time now. She says she has some- thing important to tell me.

ANDREW
Maybe old James has finally proposed.

SANDRA
That would be the day. She hinted that it was something to do with Derek and me.

ANDREW
How are things going in that direction?

SANDRA
I don't know what to say, Dad. It's all so frustrating. Everyone is getting on so funny, and well, you know for yourself how Mommy is behaving.

ANDREW
It takes a lot of courage for a single woman to have a child in our society. And going to live common law with Derek isn't going to make things any better.

SANDRA

I know that Dad, and I'm beginning to wonder if all this stress and strain is worth it.

(Pause)

Up to now Derek has not been given any explanation for why he was fired from his holiday job and now nobody else will employ him. It's all so...so...it just gets me down.

ANDREW

Why don't you just get married and done?

SANDRA

We can't do that, Dad.

ANDREW

Why not?

SANDRA

We decided long ago that we'd live together without getting married, and we're not going to change that now.

ANDREW

Even though the pressure against you is becoming unbearable?

SANDRA

We're not going to let society dictate our way of life.

ANDREW

It's impossible to live in a society and not have that society dictate your way of life.

Act II

SANDRA

Daddy, I'm not in the mood for any philosophical arguments right now. And in any case, if I even wanted to get married, Derek is dead set against the idea.

ANDREW

Well the two of you are two young people. You will find a way to work things out. Where's your mother?

SANDRA

Gone to one of her church meetings I believe. You're hungry?

ANDREW

No, I'm okay.

SANDRA

(The doorbell rings)

That must be Carol now. Answer for me please, Dad.

(She takes Andrew's shoes into bedroom. Andrew answers the door. It is Carol)

ANDREW

Hi, Carol. Come on in.

CAROL

Hello Mr. Forgerty. Nice to see you.

ANDREW

Nice to see you too. Come right in and have a seat. Sandra will be out in a minute.

CAROL

Thank you.

ANDREW

Care to join me with a brandy?

CAROL

Not right now thanks.

ANDREW

Something softer then?

CAROL

Nothing at all at the moment.

SANDRA

Hi, Carol. You met Dad before didn't you?

CAROL

Oh yes. Through James; we're quite old friends.

SANDRA

Of course, I forgot that.

CAROL

Only your mother I haven't met as yet.

SANDRA

Well, you'll meet her this afternoon. She's out now but she should be back soon.

CAROL

Good. I'm looking forward to it.

ANDREW

How are things going with you, Carol?

CAROL

Not so good recently, to tell the truth.

ANDREW

What happen, ole James not behaving himself?

CAROL

You might say so.

ANDREW

That no-good rascal.

CAROL

Would you believe I went to see him the other day and he had a woman in his bed?

ANDREW

(Laughs heartily)

That's just like James. What did the son-of-a-gun have to say for himself?

CAROL

If he even had anything to say I didn't want to hear. I wash my hands. I'm done with that!

SANDRA

That would really serve him right for true. It's just what he deserves.

ANDREW

Oh, you'll get over it.

CAROL

Not this time. I've had it up to here.

(Puts hand to neck)

And I'm not taking any more shit from him.

ANDREW

That's what you say now, but you'll get over it.

CAROL

I don't think so. When I decide to give myself to a man, it is to that man and that man alone. And I expect the same thing in return. No, I demand the same thing in return, and if he's not prepared to give it, then he doesn't deserve me.

ANDREW

But surely you must have known that Don Juan, Cassonova, and James Llewellyn Wellington are all in the same league.

CAROL

Well, it was just hearsay. And he kept giving me the assurance there was nobody else.

ANDREW

He gave you that assurance?

CAROL

Honest to God.

ANDREW

Well, why am I pretending to be surprised?

CAROL

So I went to see him one day. The same day he came back from Guyana, and he seemed happy to see me, wanted me to spend the afternoon with him and all that, but this woman, an older mature lady came by and I left. I came to see Sandra, but nobody was here so I went back by James.

CAROL

All of a sudden he's no longer happy to see me. He's making every excuse to get me to leave. But I stayed and happened to go into his bedroom, and there sprawled off in his bed is the same woman.

ANDREW

Who was the woman?

CAROL

I don't know and I don't want to know. All I know is that I felt like strangling her.

SANDRA

You should have strangled him.

CAROL

Right. So before I ended up with blood on my hands, I got out of there and out of the relationship in a lot of hurry.

ANDREW

I know you girls have other business to talk over so I'll get out of your way and let you get on with it.

SANDRA

No, Daddy, stay. I want him to hear what's happening, Carol, okay?

CAROL

Sure.

SANDRA

So…what's going down?

CAROL

Girl, I don't even know where to start. You know that old Teacher Alice who I live with is on the school board, don't you? Well she told me today that the board had a special meeting last night to discuss the situation with you and Derek.

SANDRA

Really? What they say?

CAROL

Don't say I told you, but they decided to ask for your resignation.

SANDRA

Oh my God! But why? On what grounds?

CAROL

You know how those old people think. She said your getting pregnant is bad enough, but going to live in sin with Derek makes it even ten times worse. Plus you know they have to talk about what a bad influence you will be on the children and that kind of thing.

SANDRA

Those old conceited, self-righteous, phonies! Isn't there anything I can do Dad?

ANDREW

Like what?

SANDRA

To stop them from doing it! To fight them!

ANDREW

I really don't know my dear. I would suggest you call Derek and tell him about it.

SANDRA

I don't see how that is going to help.

ANDREW

Well, it's his problem just as much as yours. Both of you work it out together.

SANDRA

(A little annoyed)

Okay, if that's the way you feel, we'll work it out ourselves.

(She exits)

CAROL

Why don't they just get married?

ANDREW

Maybe they realise marriage isn't as glorious as it is supposed to be.

CAROL

They could at least give it a try.

ANDREW

They want to try something else.

CAROL

But they can see how other people here feel about that. How are they going to get it to work?

(Andrew rubs his eye again)

CAROL

Is there something in your eye? You keep rubbing it and that's not good.

ANDREW

Yes, I think so. It's been bothering me all afternoon but whatever it is I can't seem to get it out.

CAROL

Just a minute, I'll take it out for you.

(She comes to the couch, peeps into his eye and blows into it. She is in a very suggestive position when Ann steps into the room. Ann is dumbstruck) There. How's that?

ANDREW

Good. Very good.

ANN

What is this for me at all!

CAROL

(Swinging around and seeing Ann)

You!

ANN

You? You have the nerve to come to my house messing about with my husband?

ANDREW

What the hell is the matter with you Ann? You going stupid or something?

ANN

(Almost in hysterics)

I don't what to hear anything from you!

ANDREW

What's wrong with you, woman?

ANN

Just leave me alone.

ANDREW

Ann!

ANN

I don't want to hear nothing!

(She exits)

ANDREW

Ann! What the hell kind of ass is that woman?

CAROL

Is that your wife?

ANDREW

Yes, that's my wife.

CAROL

Are you sure?

ANDREW

Sure, I'm sure. You don't think that by now I'd know my own wife?

CAROL

But…but…

ANDREW

But what?

CAROL

No. Forget it. I'm off. Tell Sandra I'll talk to her later.

ANDREW

Not at all. What is it? What's the matter?

CAROL

You don't want to hear this.

ANDREW

Sure I do. Come on, tell me what it is.

(Pause)

Come on. You can tell me.

CAROL

That's the same woman I was telling you about.

ANDREW

What woman?

CAROL

The one I saw in James' bed!

ANDREW

No. That couldn't be.

CAROL

Yes, I tell you. I saw her with my own eyes.

ANDREW

Are you sure?

CAROL

Absolutely!

ANDREW

(Thoughtful for a while)

No. You must have been mistaken.

CAROL

Well. I'm glad you think so.

SANDRA

What was that fuss all about? Where's Mommy?

ANDREW

I can't understand what's the matter with your mother. She came and met Carol taking something out of my eye, and obviously thought we were necking. So she raised a god-damn-it and stormed out of the room.

SANDRA

Oh God. Carol I'm really sorry about that. Mommy hasn't been herself these last few weeks so please don't take it badly.

CAROL

Don't worry about it. It's just that she scared the hell out of me. I could almost swear that she is the same woman I was telling you about with James.

SANDRA

Mommy? In James' bed?

CAROL

I think it was she.

SANDRA

Oh no, you must be mistaken. It couldn't possibly have been her.

CAROL

Well, if you say so.

ANDREW

Let me go and ask her.

CAROL

No, don't. I might be wrong and that will only cause more trouble. Let's just forget it.

SANDRA

That's right Dad, because I'm sure there must be a mistake. And the state Mommy is in, if you go and ask her anything like that, she's only going to flare up worse.

(Andrew shrugs)

I'm mixing some passion fruit juice. That's okay for you Carol or would you prefer something else?

CAROL

That's fine.

SANDRA

How about you, Dad?

ANDREW

I'll drink a glass of it.

SANDRA

Coming up in a minute.

79

Act II

CAROL
I really don't think I ought to stay.

ANDREW
Of course you ought to stay. Everything is going to be alright.

(The doorbell rings and Derek enters)

DEREK
Hi. What's happening?

CAROL
Hi, Derek.

DEREK
Where's Sandra?

SANDRA
I'm in the kitchen Derek. Would you like something to drink?

DEREK
Not now thanks.

(He sits)

ANDREW
It looks as if the battle is getting hot.

DEREK
So it seems.

(Sandra comes in and serves drinks to Carol and Andrew)

SANDRA
Well what you think about me getting fired?

DEREK

Somebody is definitely putting some pressure on us.

SANDRA

But who would want to do that?

DEREK

Who else? It could only be Daddy.

SANDRA

You think he would really go that far.

DEREK

You don't know him. But I could smell his hand in this. It's funny the way I lost my job just so. And you losing your job now makes it look even fishier. I thought the days of firing pregnant teachers were long over.

SANDRA

Why is life so full of trouble?

ANDREW

The way I see it, you're responsible for all the trouble you're having. All you have to do is get married and your troubles disappear. Of course new ones will arise, but you'll deal with those when they appear.

DEREK

You're the last person I expected that kind of talk from, Andrew. You know we are dead set against the idea of marriage, and I thought you were sympathetic with our views. We can't just run off and get married now.

ANDREW

Why? Afraid of losing face? Too proud to back down? Unable to change your position although common sense says you should? Man, that's a silly attitude that cripples a lot of people.

DEREK

That's the thing that's crippling the whole world. Always the easiest way out. Why doesn't society change? Why doesn't society accept change?

ANDREW

Ah, it does. But it takes ages, generations! You can't afford to wait that long.

DEREK

The change has got to start somewhere.

ANDREW

The way I see it boy, you're crippled before you even start. You don't have any money, you don't have a job, and now Sandra is about to lose her job. You're endangering your future, Sandra's future and the baby's future. Is that what you want to do?

(Long pause)

Look at it this way.

(He rests his hand on Derek's shoulder)

Why don't you get married...

(Derek shakes off his hand)

ANDREW

...for the moment, just for the moment. That'll take the heat off both of you for a while.

82

ANDREW (Continued)

Sandra will be able to keep her job, and you'd be able to finish school. After you graduate and establish yourself, you can divorce each other and live happily ever after.

SANDRA

Oh Daddy. Can't you ever be serious?

ANDREW

But I am serious. I'm very serious.

SANDRA

You make a joke out of everything.

DEREK

Now wait a minute, that's a good idea. As a matter of fact, that's a damn good idea!

ANDREW

Of course it's a good idea.

DEREK

The best.

ANDREW

(Merrily)

Well, let's fire one on it.

SANDRA

Derek, you really serious?

(She comes up to Derek whose attitude has changed to one of playful humor. He embraces her and swings around with her. Then with a mocking bow)

DEREK

Fair damsel, light of my life, leading lady in all my dreams, will you marry me?

(He is about to kiss her hand. but his mood has spread to her, so she pulls it scornfully away)

SANDRA

Away! Filthy peasant. How dare you think of proposing to a lady of my esteem without a white convertible and a suit of purest silk?

(They all laugh)

ANDREW

(Putting an arm around Derek's shoulder)

Me thinks the lady doth protest too much. How sayest thou we slip away to yon Yacht Club for a drink or two?

DEREK

Splendid proposition my dear fellow, splendid.

(Andrew starts leading Derek away. After they have taken two or three steps towards the door, Sandra rushes and puts an arm across Derek's shoulder so he is between herself and Andrew. She is stage right and Andrew is stage left. Their backs are to the audience)

SANDRA

Oh no you don't.

(She swings them around so that all three are facing the audience. She is now stage left and Andrew is stage right)

SANDRA (Continued)

The two of you are staying right here. Why don't you get some ice from the kitchen and fix drinks for all of us while I tell Mommy the news.

(She gives them a gentle push)

DEREK

(Humorously to Andrew)

You see? She's not even married to me as yet and she's pushing me around already.

(They move towards the kitchen)

SANDRA

Carol. I hope you know you've got to be one of my bridesmaids.

DEREK & ANDREW

(Derek and Andrew pause at the kitchen door because of what Sandra has said. They look at each other and shake their heads. Then throwing up their hands in a gesture of resignation, they say as they exit)

Women, women, women!

CAROL

I'm so happy for you, dear.

SANDRA

I'm so relieved myself. Let me call Mommy.

(Going to the door)

Mommy! Come on out and hear the news. Wait until she hears!

CAROL
Look, I'm going to go give the boys a hand in the kitchen.

(She exits)

SANDRA
Mommy, come here a minute.

ANN
(From inside)

What are you annoying me for child?

SANDRA
Derek and I are going to get married!

ANN
(Appearing quickly)

What you say?

SANDRA
Derek and I are getting married.

ANN
Oh thank you Jesus. I know you'd never let me down.

(She embraces Sandra)

Thank you Jesus, thank you.

(Releasing Sandra)

When did you decide?

SANDRA
Just now.

ANN

What a weight has been lifted off me this night. The Lord really hears and answers prayers. Oh give thanks unto the Lord for he is just and his mercies endureth forever. Thank you my Jesus, thank you. You told your father?

SANDRA

Of course.

ANN

What he say?

SANDRA

He's happy.

ANN

And where he gone to now?

SANDRA

In the kitchen.

ANN

Let me get him in here

(She exits, returns immediately, takes hold of Sandra's hand and leads her down right)

What is she still doing here?

SANDRA

That reminds me. How could you let yourself be carried away like that this afternoon, Mommy?

ANN

What you wanted me to do? If I come in and see her...

87

SANDRA

See what! All she was doing was taking something out of Daddy's eye.

ANN

That's what they tell you. But I saw them with my own two eyes.

SANDRA

Oh, Mommy! You really think she would be kissing Daddy knowing I'd just gone into the kitchen to come back in a minute?

ANN

You were here with them?

SANDRA

Of course I was here. I had just gone into the kitchen to get us something to drink. Daddy came home complaining about something in his eye and I had even tried getting it out myself.

ANN

Well, I didn't realise all of this.

SANDRA

I think you owe her an apology, Mommy.

ANN

Owe her what apology?

SANDRA

Please. She's my good friend and I don't want this to get between us. Okay?

ANN

Well, if you say so.

SANDRA

(Going to kitchen for Carol)

Carol, come a minute please.

(Carol enters)

Carol, this is my mother. Mommy, Carol Summersdale.

ANN

Hello.

CAROL

Hello.

ANN

This afternoon I was bit upset and…and, I didn't realize…I hope you understand.

CAROL

Oh, don't worry about it. I've forgotten it already.

ANDREW

(He enters with Derek. They bring on bottles of liquor, some coke and some ginger ale, glasses and a bucket of ice)

The drinks are here.

ANN

Oh Derek, I'm so overjoyed. I always knew that at heart you were a good boy and would do what is right and proper. Has anybody phoned your father to tell him as yet?

DEREK

I hope not. I'm not too anxious for him to hear.

ANN

Why not? I'm going to call him up right now and tell him.

(She is on her way when Andrew calls out)

ANDREW

Wait a minute Ann. Just wait a minute. Were you over at James' place a few days ago?

ANN

Er...er...yes. I went to find out about the wedding.

ANDREW

Then what the hell were you doing in his bed?

ANN

Well...I...er...

DEREK

I put her there, Andrew. What's the matter with you, getting jealous in your old age? She had one of her dizzy spells and passed out. Dad's room was the clos-est, so I took her in there to rest for a while.

ANDREW

So that's what happened.

CAROL

That explains it! When I went into the bedroom and saw her there, I put more to it than there really was. Well I guess it's my turn to apologise.

ANN

Let's just cast it aside and forget about it. But you, Andrew! You mean to tell me that your mind is so far in the gutter and so…

SANDRA

Mommy! Just go and make the call please and don't start another quarrel.

ANN

No. You better come with me and make the call, Carol. I'll get supper ready for all of us.

CAROL

That's a good idea. When I'm finished with the call I'll give you a hand.

(They start to exit)

ANDREW

Hey, Carol, I thought it was all over between you and James.

CAROL

Let's just call this one a close shave, shall we?

(She exits)

ANDREW

That man has more lives than a cat.

(He pours drinks for Sandra, Derek, and himself)
Here's to good luck, good health, happiness and long life!

SANDRA

Here, here.

DEREK

Cheers.

(Derek and Carol speak as they all clink glasses. They drink)

SANDRA

I hope everything will go smoothly now.

ANDREW

I don't see why it shouldn't.

DEREK

You know, I don't think I want Daddy to be in any way involved with this wedding.

SANDRA

But why?

DEREK

His attitude bugs me.

SANDRA

You're only annoyed because he threw you out the house.

DEREK

It's not only that. He needs to learn that he can't always have things his own way. He can't continue to push his weight around without any regards for other people.

SANDRA

You're just rationalizing Derek. He appears to be coming out on top in this little battle, and that's all that's eating you. You could at least let him win this time, for a change.

DEREK

I'm not rationalizing! Well maybe I am, a little bit.

SANDRA

Of course you are. You can't bear to have him think that he has gotten the best of you.

DEREK

(On whom the booze is beginning to take slight effect)

You're damn right. Anyway, what the heck! If the wedding is on, I suppose he might as well enjoy it too…while it lasts. Eh, Andrew?

ANDREW

(Who is also beginning to feel the effects of the drinks)

You sure don't have anything to lose. He's going to be so overjoyed to have you back home, that he'll kill the fatted calf. Hell, he'll kill a dozen fatted calves.

DEREK

Well if he wants to be impressive, he better kill the whole damn herd.

ANDREW

I'll drink to that.

ANN

(Entering)

How you all mean to tell me that you can plan such an evil, wicked, sinful thing as divorce, before you all even get married!?

93

SANDRA & DEREK

What?

ANN

Yes, Carol just told me.

ANDREW

For chrissake, Ann…

ANN

And you Andrew, you sit by…

SANDRA

Mommy. Just calm down and let me explain everything to you.

ANN

Explain and explain good, because I will not be part of any mockery.

(The doorbell rings long and loudly)

ANDREW

That has to be James.

(He takes hold of Ann and puts her to sit beside him)

Sit down and keep your mouth shut, Ann.

(The doorbell is heard again. Sandra opens it. A beaming James steps in)

JAMES

Congratulations! Congratulations! How's everybody?

SANDRA

Great! We're sort of sitting around waiting for you to get here.

JAMES

(Giving her a hug)

Ah, you're going to make me a fine daughter-in-law. I came over as soon as I heard the good news. Come on, Molly, take those things into the kitchen and see if you can manage to make yourself useful.

(Molly enters burdened with two huge shopping bags of food stuff and goes into the kitchen)

Nice to know you have come to your senses, my boy. Joe, where the hell are you with the champagne, man?

JOE

(From outside)

Coming right up, sah.

(Joe enters with a case of Champagne)

SANDRA

A case of champagne?

JAMES

Well is not every day this boy of mine comes to his senses and gets married to a pretty little girl like you. We got to celebrate the occasion in grand style.

ANDREW

Fine! Fire one in the meantime.

JAMES

Good idea. Pour your father-in-law a scotch and ginger, my dear. Well, Ann, what did I tell you? What did I tell you, Andrew? Didn't I say I would personally see to it that everything works out fine?

ANDREW
How did you manage it?

JAMES
Trade secret, my friend, trade secret. But you know how it is with me. I have my way of handling these ticklish little problems. When I make a promise. I make a debt. And after all, never let it be said that I, James Llewellyn Wellington, ever made a debt that I didn't honor.

DEREK
Go ahead and gloat, Daddy. Gloat your head off.

JAMES
What the devil are you talking about?

DEREK
You know damn well what I'm talking about. I'm talking about you turning the screws on me. I'm talking about you getting me fired and blocking me from getting hired anyplace else. And no doubt you had a little chat with the school board and had Sandra fired too. Jesus Christ Daddy!

JAMES
Don't let it upset you son. Things are going to work out just fine.

(Offering his hand)

No hard feelings.

DEREK
(Slapping the hand away)

Like hell no hard feelings!

SANDRA

(Intercepting with a drink)

Please, please! No more quarreling, please.

JAMES

(Taking a drink)

You're quite right my dear. We've had enough of those, the two of us. Listen, Derek. Let's reason this thing out. Getting married isn't going to hurt you. You're going to have a nice wife, who I'll arrange to have transferred to Jamaica so she can be with you while you finish school. But if you had gone to live in sin, you would be asking me to change my values of what is right and what is wrong.

DEREK

(With an ironical sneer)

Your values of what is right and what is wrong?

JAMES

I know you young people have your own modern ideas of how to live life, and I'm not saying that you all are wrong. But after all, I'm an old man now, and it's easier to destroy old men than to change them. And if you had gone and done what you were planning, you would not only be destroying me, but yourself and Sandra, and the reputation of the whole Forgerty family.

DEREK

Amen, brother, amen! You maybe able to con the rest of the world, Dad, but I know well enough that the only criterion you have of right and wrong, is what brings you votes and what doesn't.

JAMES

Surprised at you my boy. Surprised at you. Don't be giving away my trade secrets like that in public. Well, what the hell. We're all one big family now, so there should be no secrets between us anyway. And take it from me, Derek, by getting married to Sandra, you're doing absolutely the right thing.

DEREK

One of these days, Dad, one of these days...

(They embrace)

JAMES

Come on, give us some music somebody. We have an engagement to celebrate. Ann, how come you're so glum. Cheer up. Call up some friends and let's get this celebration going.

ANN

(Getting up)

No. My conscience couldn't let me go through with it. Oh, Mr. Wellington, this is only a sinful, wicked, evil trick.

JAMES

What the devil are you talking about?

ANN

They are planning to divorce one another as soon as Derek gets out of school.

SANDRA

Mommy, for heaven's sake, don't be so silly. After all the trouble we've been through, you think we'd want

SANDRA (Continued)

to go through it all again with a divorce? The mere thoughts of how you and Mr. James Llewellyn Wellington are going to carry on, is enough to change even the devil's mind. Besides, divorces are so expensive that I'm sure it's not going to be worth it.

ANN

Don't listen to her, Mr. Wellington! They have it all figured out.

JAMES

Anything go like this?

ANDREW

Come, come. Let's not cross our bridges before we get to them.

JAMES

Well said, well said. We'll deal with that when and if the time comes. Right now we have the engagement and then the wedding.

(To Sandra)

Try out the marriage business for yourself and see what it's like. If you don't like it, then...we'll see. But, before you go and do anything stupid, see to it that you give me some healthy grandchildren. Legitimate ones too.

SANDRA

Just see to it that you don't get yourself destroyed too soon.

JAMES

(Laughing)

JAMES (Continued)

Don't worry about that. Your old father-in-law is harder to sink than a battleship.

(Calling)

Where's the champagne!

(Molly enters from kitchen with glasses of champagne on a tray. She serves each person. When she gets to Ann, Ann hesitates)

ANDREW

Go on, Ann. Have one for the stomachs sake.

ANN

Well, I suppose I might as well.

(She takes a drink and downs it)

For the stomach's sake.

JAMES

Joe, get in here and have some champagne. Have a glass too, Molly.

(Joe enters)

JAMES

Where's the music around here?

(Sandra puts on some hot calypso music. At the same time, Carol enters from the kitchen with a tray of hors d'oeuvres. James takes the tray from her, puts it on the centre table and they start to dance. Derek and Sandra dance. Molly and Joe dance. By and by, Andrew and Ann do a jig. They all continue to dance as the lights fade to black)

THE END

www.ingramcontent.com/pod-product-compliance
Lightning Source LLC
Chambersburg PA
CBHW071556040426
42452CB00008B/1193